JUG BAND JAG

Kit Wright was born in 1944 in Crockham Hill, Kent, and has published widely for adults and children. After a scholarship to Oxford, he worked as a lecturer in Canada, was education officer at the Poetry Society from 1970 to 1975, Fellow Commoner in the Creative Arts at Trinity College, Cambridge in 1977-79, and subsequently a freelance writer. His poetry titles include *The Bear Looked Over the Mountain* (Salamander, 1977), *Bump-Starting the Hearse* (Hutchinson, 1983), *Poems 1974-1983* (Hutchinson, 1988), *Short Afternoons* (Hutchinson, 1989), *Hoping It Might Be So: Poems 1974-2000*, including new collection (Leviathan, 2000; Faber, 2008), *Ode to Didcot Power Station* (Bloodaxe Books, 2014) and *Jug Band Jag* (Bloodaxe Books, 2025). A selection of his poems was included in *Penguin Modern Poets 1* (second series, 1995). He has won many literary awards, including the Geoffrey Faber Memorial Prize, Alice Hunt Bartlett Prize, Hawthornden Prize, Heinemann Award and Cholmondeley Award.

KIT WRIGHT

Jug Band Jag

BLOODAXE BOOKS

www.bloodaxebooks.com
For further information about Bloodaxe titles
please visit our website and join our mailing list
or write to the above address for a catalogue.

Supported using public funding by
**ARTS COUNCIL
ENGLAND**

Cover design: Neil Astley & Pamela Robertson-Pearce.

Printed in Great Britain by Bell & Bain Limited, 303 Burnfield Road,
Thornliebank, Glasgow G46 7UQ, Scotland, on acid-free paper
sourced from mills with FSC chain of custody certification.

For Marianne

ACKNOWLEDGEMENTS

Some of these poems have previously been published in *The Spectator*. 'Torpedo Path' is much indebted to Alan Wren's superb account of the disaster, *The Ambush of SS Persia: Voices from a Lost Liner* (2020).

CONTENTS

ONE

Namesake

It might be a long, long time since I was christened Christopher
And nicknamed Kit…but not so long ago
As 1570, when was born my namesake,
Who did his best to stage the Fireworks Show

That nearly happened. Yet they blew their chance
And came to grief, as which of us wouldn't have done?
Myself, I'd have been particularly useless,
Managing of the manoeuvres only one:

Cloaked and daggered, meeting my co-conspirators
For a conspiratorial drink in the Duck and Drake
Off Fleet Street. I'd have been first man at the bar.
That part of the Plot I'd have found a piece of cake.

But nothing involving mental or physical courage,
Enduring the third degree, to the slightest degree.
There again, sociopathic terrorism
On such a scale might not have appealed to me,

I hope. But once you were in you were stuck with the Just
And Glorious Enterprise – no turning back
For Catesby, Wintour, Percy, Fawkes and of course,
The indispensable Wright Brothers, Kit and Jack.

The following day, they rode like hell through the rain
To get to the Staffordshire safe house, where the entire
Project collapsed through yet more gunpowder ordnance –
Which colleagues decided to dry out by the fire.

Inexplicably, it exploded. Damaged
Beyond repair, they staggered out to be shot
By the Sheriff of Worcester's posse, as in a western.
And so Kit Wright was released from the Gunpowder Plot.

They were martial Catholics, soldiers of Spain, Yorkshiremen,
And apart from other bondings, brothers-in-law.
They were persecuted and they had been betrayed
And terrors rained down on the innocent as before.

A Pub Wall in 1974

Thinking about those nights
   Kindles a strange felicity:
Drinking by candlelight
   In a pub off the Earls Court Road
In the time of the Three Day Week,
   Because there was no electricity.

Certainly we were political.
   Nothing, though, seemed as serious –
Intimate and critical –
   As the play our shadows made,
Taking their parts in the dance
   Of things made newly mysterious.

As in a diorama
   Device of antique design,
The scene flickered with meanings
   We never knew we possessed:
Each stranger having a guest
   Role in the psychodrama.

Serious, yes, and also
   Childlike too, in a way:
Like a treat, like a bedtime story
   Told in that shadow play:
Chiaroscuro, likewise, its themes,
   The dangerous dark and the glory

Of flame. We were not so much
   Aligned with that time and place
As we were somehow in touch
   With the only model that fits:
The company of forerunners,
   The breathing ghosts of the Blitz.

One Item or Less

Poetry wasn't my first love,
Said the pale man in the public bar
Of the *Human Condition*. No,
Poetry wasn't my first love:
My first love was dry cleaning.

What?

For I come from a long line
Of practitioners of that mystery,
And certain things are in my blood:
The tang of the chemical fluid,
The gossamer whisper of polythene,
Scrape and slide of hangers
Riding the rails. I guess
As a child I drank them in,
The magic and the romance…

Please.

There was nothing I loved more
Than to hang around the machines,
Hearing the yarns of the old
Dry cleaning heroes.

For Christsake.

They held me
Spellbound, like the momentum
Of the cabinet itself,
Whose one eye, ever-rolling,
First taught me the world was round.

Quite young, I won a franchise
And assumed my first command
On a stony reach of the Suffolk
Coast, as flat and straight
As a trouser crease – except
For the terraces of shingle
That rolled twice to the sea.
My Sketchleys
Plied a diminishing trade
On that desolate shelf of land,
As the last commercial undertaking
Alive on the promenade.

And then

She was standing by the counter,
A small woman,
Her face somehow compounded
Of the wind and the stones on the shore:
A woman along the lines
Of a little boy with stone-coloured eyes
And a raspberry-coloured woollen hat.
She'd an old suitcase in tow
(Containing who knew what garment?)
Then the phone rang out the back.
I got it, and when I returned,
She'd gone. The wind was mixing it
With the jumbo breakers harrumphing in,
It was raining hard in the sea
And the unforgiving afternoon
Darkened and darkened. The storm
Cracked open, and all the time
The machine was crafting its own
Weather, its little paradigm
Of turbulence and re-shaping,
Its manic exposition
In whine and whirr and drum-roll. Then

Behind the glass I caught
A seam of red in the melange
And knew it for the woolly hat,
Disconnected. And then
Her face came staring by
And I jumped across
And stopped the machine,
I stopped the bloody thing.
But there was nothing there,
I mean nothing untoward until
The suitcase began to cry.
It was just about alive,
The baby, when the ambulance came.
And then I got into poetry,
Terza rima, heroic couplets,
Lyrics and sonnets, ballads and blues,
But it wasn't my first love,
It wasn't my first
Love.

The Art of Adolf Hitler

a pendular rhymepiece

People do not care to be rejected:
A simple truth about the human race.
And Hitler, well before he was selected
As Chancellor, presents a striking case.
It wasn't Nazidom that he directed
His first ambitions at, to build his base,
But *German* Socialism – which detected
In Adolf Hitler just a waste of space.
So when in time a union was projected
Between the parties, Hitler set his face
Against the plan which, had it been effected,
Might have defused…at least have slowed the pace.

But years before, his ego disrespected
When Art School turned him down, he felt disgrace,
Humiliation. He was disconnected…
If only they had let him in the place.

The Ambition of Joe Aiello
Or The Fifty-Nine Slugs

Giusepp' Aiello
Was a very persistent fellow.

As a noted Chicago resident,
He had long aspired to be President

Of Unione Siciliana,
But was always second banana.

It made him sadder and sadder
That others surmounted the greasy ladder,

But he himself
Was forever stuck on the shelf

Below.
Joe

Did not reflect
That those the Unione deigned to elect

To the topmost post
Were toast

Almost straight away.
He thought the prospects OK.

So of course he was disappointed
When other heads were anointed,

But if these were perchance blown off,
He'd simply scoff:

'When the job's mine,
Security will be fine.'

But three bullets entered the brain
Of Angelo Genna, curtailing his reign,

And no sooner
Had Samoots Amatuna

Taken the palm
Than he suffered identical harm.

Was the position hexed?
Tony Lombardo was next

And I'm sorry to say
He immediately passed away.

Then Patsy Lolordo was able
To get to the head of the table

For a brief appearance
Before his…clearance…

In the same manner.
And then –

HOSANNA!

GLORY BE!
At last the position was free!

His Destiny set in stone,
Giuseppe ascended the Throne…

* * * * *

Was it long and contented,
His time at the helm?

Did he widen his borders,
Expand his realm?

No.
Unfortunately this wasn't so.

Death gave its approval
For his removal.

No less than fifty-nine slugs
Were inserted in him by a minion of Bugs

Or else by a pal
Of Al.

Extracted, these weighed
A pound and a half

And constitute
His epitaph.

Shadoof

Ancient Egyptians put to proof,
Along the never-ending Nile,
The virtues of the old shadoof
And plied the same in fulcrum style.

The Bronze Age engineer, no goof,
Would fix the counterpoint with care,
As though he ran the warp and woof
Of water by a shuttle there.

Rock on, rock on, you old shadoof,
Your bucket full, your balance true!
Five thousand years to man's behoof:
For all the world as good as new.

Birch

When she planted the silver birch at the end
Of the garden, all those years ago,
She taped a coin to its single branch
To weigh it down and make it spread.

Did somebody call the birch
A trinketty kind of tree?
Up yer arse with a ragman's trumpet!

It's tough as old boots
Which they used to make from it;
Tough as old boats
Which they made from it too.

Bloody-minded enough to be first
To stab its way out of the Ice Age. So

We might drink its wine,
Burn its logs,
Smoke and distil with it,
Carve and write on it,
Sleep on it, build ourselves a home:

Praising always its tender solidity,
Praising its ribbony satin
Radiance,

Chronicle of our London clay:
Our whispers at its catkin tips,
Our cries in its torn pages.

The Bird Itself

Easy to recognise because it no longer
Breeds in Dartford,
The Dartford Warbler

Has dark red underparts: not underpants,
As once was thought. Its song
Is a harsh Ker-rist, Ker-rist,

From under a dustbin.
Its habitat
Is wild or semi-wild heathland, or the blocked

Vents of central heating systems
During reports at Annual General Meetings.
It lends its name

To an unusual magazine,
The Warbler,
Not produced in Dartford:

No longer, in fact, available anywhere.
But once it served a community
Or pack of a sort,

A feral
Readership of nine
Who kept a strict control

Of editorial policy. *The Warbler*
Cheeped in a strangulated manner
Not entirely unlike the bird itself.

Creation Song of Westgate

1

Hardly a man is now alive
Who knows that in 1865 *

Westgate-on-Sea was yet unborn
And fields of sprouts and standing corn

Extended to the main:

There were no gravelled avenues
Crunched by discriminating shoes:

No pulpit held the plain...

Until, as destiny required,

The cavalcade
   Of waves inspired
The blue parade
   And boulevard
The promenade
   And esplanade
And Westgate made
   A taut resort
   Contingent on the sea...

   It kitted out
      A neat retreat
   It fitted out
      A STOUT REDOUBT

   To face the wild North Sea.

*Thanks to Longfellow

2

Hardly a woman's still in place
Who knows that in the year of grace

Eighteen hundred and sixty-six
Was laid the first of the Kentish bricks

Composed in part of coke,

That lent distinction to the scheme
That reified the founders' dream

And Westgate Town awoke…

And then, as some far star desired,

The cavalcade
    Of waves inspired
The blue parade
    And boulevard
The promenade
    And esplanade
And Westgate made
    A taut resort
Contingent on the sea…

    It kitted out
        A neat retreat
    It fitted out
        A STOUT REDOUBT

To face the wild North Sea.

3

Let Herman Mertens, developer,
Stand on the land he's acutely acquired
And gaze back up the estuary
As far as the Isle of Sheppey
And the ghost of the Isle of Grain.

Thanet, the hipbone of the South,
Is where he stands. An island once,
Cleft by the Wantsum Channel,
Favoured seaway of the Romans,
Silted up five hundred years.
And now the Railway's due
To follow the Roman helmets: this
Is the golden key to Herman's
Speculative punt.
He will sell it on (the whole Estate
Will be sold on many times) but for now
It's Herman's oyster. It won't
Be boisterous and salty
Like Margate down the road,
Nor louche like France around the corner,
Nor Belgian like Belgium nearby.
It will be exclusive, excluding
As many as possible while providing
A second home, a country home
For the Metropolitan Gentleman,
To fill his lungs with the high sea-wind
Through the timeliness of Steam.
Featureless, except for the sea,
And historically anonymous,
Here is the perfect *tabula rasa*
On which the gated imagination
May print its dreams – and of course,
A clean slate for the disparaged
And a fresh playground for hope.

4

Well, of course it was the exclusive
Who spoiled the scheme by excluding themselves
In rather too generous numbers.
But look, it's the great Erasmus Wilson
Who takes the first four bungalows!
President of the Royal
College of Surgeons, dermatological
Supersage and liberal spirit…
Father of syphilis studies
And prophet of hydrotherapy,
Plus:
Egyptological benefactor
Who paid for Cleopatra's Needle
To sail from Alexandria! This

Excellent friend of the poor
Now lighted upon the strange and favoured
Settlement to receive
His advocacy of clean sea air
And seawater baths
Piped in from the bay.
And so in dozens and dozens
Of rigorous private hotels
That sprang up instantaneously
Along the chill front, at his will,
Balconies bloomed with beds
Containing purple-faced
Convalescents,
Cured, or of course
The opposite,
As nature deemed it best.

5

Early too was the advent
Of a certain discreet bohemianism,
At odds with the township's
Reputation
For frigid respectability
And toffee-nosed
Up it self-
Regard.
(Unfair, perhaps, but at one time,
Over twenty prep schools
Chirruped into the wind.) The arts
Were represented by Scottish painters –
With William Quiller Orchardson
Heading the field of residents.
His narrative scenes depicted
Quandaries and showdowns,
Bouleversements and *froideurs*.
Le Mariage de Convenance takes
An old man's darling
Sulking at her aged spouse
From the opposite end of a mile-long table,
Nemesis looming. Would this be
A selfie of the Orchardsons' own
Marriage, with twenty years between them?

Mais au contraire, they adored each other!

6

And at the end of his life she led him
Painfully down to the final canvas,
Held him steady while he touched in
The last brush-stroke
He would ever make. His work
Was finished.

She never let him know
There would be no money left for her.
Everything had gone
And the picture of prosperity
She had painted for his comfort
Was a fiction like his art.
Her widowhood was straitened
As her love had not been.

7

But that was the future, and London.
St Mildreds Bay was here and now
And tingled with promise. The Orchardson children
Sped on the flowering cliffs to Birchington,
Clambered down over the boulders to find
The blind sea speaking in lost caves,
Only to them. On the chalk bluffs,
Oracular groves of holly-oaks,
Salt clumps of alexanders. The house
Was a shakeable box of pieces
That landed in whimsical combinations:
Banjo-players, actors, astronomers,
Real Tennis champions (they'd built themselves
An open-air court),
The leading conjurers in the land
And its worst equestrian, Linley Sambourne.

Round and short, this *Punch* cartoonist,
Sure enough on a horse named Punch,
Would ride along the sands to see them
All the way from Ramsgate. Dressed
In a white suit trimmed with sky-blue piping
And tam o' shanter, without fail
He fell off Punch and into the sea
When they turned for the Orchardsons
At journey's end. Of such
Mishaps is happiness made
For children and forever.

8

Good luck, then, to the maverick
    And self-created town,
From which no local fleet put out
    To hunt the herring down:

No great sea-battle ever
    Bled out in the bay,
And Canterbury Pilgrims took
    A different Pilgrims Way.

One risible class system
    Stood by as standing joke
The year *Das Kapital* appeared
    And Westgate Town awoke.

9

Will there be anyone left alive
In dear old twenty-one sixty-five

To celebrate Westgate's triple ton?
Or will its earthly race be run

And in St Mildreds Bay

Nothing but plastic seal the sand
To choke the Author by whose hand

The town came into play?

When by what strange compulsion fired,

The cavalcade
   Of waves inspired
The blue parade
   And boulevard
The promenade
   And esplanade
And Westgate made
   A taut resort
Contingent on the sea...

   It kitted out
     A neat retreat
   It fitted out
     A STOUT REDOUBT

   To face the wild North Sea.

Halfway Round the Golf Course

1

Half-way round the golf-course,
The club professional, Reg,
Begged leave to offer a wedge
To Mrs Gedge.

'If you're agreeable,
I'll give you an excellent wedge
Behind that hedge.'

But of course she was NOT agreeable.

And this was entirely foreseeable.

2

Half-way round the golf course,
The club professional, Taffy,
Begged leave to offer a baffy
To Mrs Macnafee.

'If you're amenable,
I'll give you a fine baffy
Behind the café.'

But of course she was NOT amenable.

So the meeting was unconvenable.

At the Walter Pater Hogroast

At the Walter Pater Hogroast,
Loudly groaned the Ethereal Choir
Newman's harsh Apologetics –
Then the Reader in Aesthetics,
Tearing off his hi vis jacket,
Hurled his tankard on the fire.

'I will fight the hardest Aesthete,
Man or Woman, in the room!
This choir sucks at Hermeneutics.
Just you bloody wait! In two ticks,
When I get to be Professor,
Lilies will be back in bloom!

MUSCULAR AESTHETICISM:
All the other stuff is shit!
Bring another barrel, feller,
Glug it down and toast the YELLER
BOOK, and why not chuck another
Hog, for Christsake, on the spit?'

Guest House Threats

The woman who puts down fourteen quarts of Beef Tea every day,
The fellow who's just as good as his word...and hasn't a word to say,
The Vicar who doesn't believe in God but hates Him anyway,

They're coming to stay.

The woman whose wife is a hybrid form of speaking indoor plant,
The man who ate his uncle as an *amuse-bouche* for his aunt,
The thing that dares the impossible and strangely finds it can't,

They're coming to stay,
They're coming to stay,
They're coming to stay.

The League of Human Dog Thinkalikes, they're booked in for a week,
To frisk about and wag their tails and bark instead of speak,
They may not pique your interest but they'll interest your Peke,

And they're coming to stay.

The sometime Toast of Broadway who today alas is toast,
She's represented by the ghost of a ghost within a ghost,
You have to guess which ghost can boast the post of Ghost-the-Most,

They're coming to stay,
They're coming to stay,
They're coming to stay.

The Family Solicitor who appends a codicil
In his own stupendous interest to the foot of the old Lord's will
And simultaneously submits a murderous legal bill,

He's coming to stay.

The weatherwoman who warrants even worse will come to pass,
The singular vegan butcher who contends all flesh is grass,
The Emeritus Professor, who merits a kick up the arse,

They're coming to stay,
They're coming to stay,
They're coming to stay.

Black Rod is bringing the Chief Whip to stravaig and gallivant,
And one of them is a pirate and the other's a flagellant,
And each is a rooftop wrestler and a corridor corybant,

And they're coming to stay.

The Funeral Director who directs the dead to rise,
The Consultant Ophthalmologist who can't believe his eyes,
The Wholly Fatuous Concept on its way to hoist the Prize,

They're coming to stay,
They're coming to stay,
They're coming to stay.

The bloke who's on the blower to the monsters of the deep,
The specially gifted hypnotist who puts himself to sleep,
The Lord Chancellor dragging his woolsack and the actual sponsor sheep,

They're coming to stay,
Yes, come what may,
They're coming *today*!

Dead Bullet

a post mortem reconfigured

The bullet is lying in the deep muscle of the right side of the tongue.
The entry wound was below the angle of the left shoulder blade.
Between the ninth and tenth rib upwards it travelled, piercing the lung,
And passing out of the chest cavity opposite the spine.
Through the aorta, across the trachea, subsequently it made
Its way up the right side of the neck. Thus, on the appointed line,
Uncompromisingly billeted, unchastened as unsung,
The bullet is lying in the deep muscle of the right side of the tongue.

Down the Grove

Would three trees be the minimum
to constitute a grove?
Well then, a grove it is:
the triangle of turkey oaks
aligned in London Fields,
and therefore qualified to house
an Oracle.

Which ought to be a Delphi
or Dodona for
dog-owners.
For

well the dog-folk know
by the rustling of the leaves,
the Sybil is about
her inexplicably respected
mystery:
her wooden ambiguities,
her heads-you-lose
and tails-I-win
inert prognostications.

Still,
people do like secrets.
They'll go some way to make them
not entirely vacuous.

Just suppose
a dog-bloke puts the question
'How shall fare the day with my hound?'
and the answer comes,
'Your hound will take the lead today, haha'

everyone deems it sharply *apropos*,
and one up for the Oracle.
Which it isn't.

The Spirit of Alfred Tennyson Suddenly Rounds on Ezra Pound

'Pull down thy vanity thyself,
   Thou trumped-up, jumped-up *pasticheur*!
Thou monumental mountebank!
   Thou kleptomaniac *poseur*!
   Voleur!'

Las Cabras Son Malas

here come the billygoats down the track so
heavily hung with dongs that dangle
down in the dust and balls that swing
from side to side to clonkerty bells
that roll and toll on their necks the melody

ripples into the stone pine fragrance
cypress shadows the nannies plunging
onward struggling big with milk so
heavily hung with lolloping mammaries

yobs go head to head engage
in clouting rebuttals crashing the valley
all afternoon and the goatherd Gerrero
fords the ceaseless rivers of goatspiss
shouting *las cabras son malas*

A Seashell Sings

the voice of a client

The British Virgin Islands lie
    Aloof from corporation tax.
Particulars they don't supply:
    Their purpose is to cover tracks.

And just 400,000 strong,
    The companies that there abide!
To that brave host I too belong
    And offshorewise, review the tide.

Adoptive sands! Adoptive foam!
    Adoptive guardians to me!
I wouldn't change my second home
    For all the plastic in the sea.

The Forsaken Hero

The hero stood in utter desolation
On the bare shore. He wouldn't have believed
Them capable of this abomination,
His warriors – yet he had been deceived
And now his glory down the sunset died.
With everything he owned they sailed away:
His spoils, his girl, his honour and his pride:
He saw them vanishing across the bay.
Yet was there not some verbal formulation,
Some trope of rhetoric that might assuage
His anguish and his raw humiliation,
His quasi-godlike Achillean rage?
There was. At last, remembering the key word,
Into the wind he roared the plural C-word.

Arrival of the Butcher's Van in the School Drive

Time, Butcher's Van, that I began
    To hymn you panegyrically!
When at your wheels the gravel pinged
And tingled, no van, were it *winged*,
    Could have arrived more lyrically!
We marked the man vacate you, Van,
    To hob and nob satirically
With maid and cook, produce the book
    To sign as proof, empirically,
        Of how he'd made the drop
        Of chuck and blade and chop.

And so

Goodbye to the shrilling of children,
The honking of jovial women admirers;
The pungent trays are re-racked
In the back of the motor. Down
The mossy-banked drive, the butcher's
Away in the butcher's van, and swinging
On to the well-sprung lane,
As he lengthens his stride with a pinch
Of judicious acceleration.
Hedgerows go singing by, entwined
With travellers' joy and starred with stitchwort.
The Pilgrims' Way
Unreels before him, the bucking Downs
Are ramping him up and dipping him under,
The butcher barrels along
In the racketing butcher's van; the sun
Watches his progress with interest
Like a headmaster. The birds
Explete in the thorn trees at his advent;
Far away,

You can hear the tipper lorries
Double-de-clutch in painful tilting
At Westerham Hill. And here the jaunty,
Jouncing wagon is down from the ridge
And slowing, slowing into the verge.
The van is at rest like a sleeping
Dog on its heartbeat. The butcher
Opens the rear doors to the wind
And a blood breath climbs the sky.
In the copse by the chalk-stream pool
He strips and enters the grassy water,
The sunlit skeins of freezing water:
Over he rolls, he plunges under:
He swings on his back like a side of beef
On a hook, and all his sins
Are washed away…

The Migraine Show

Suddenly what we see
Appears to be just half of things

Flattened into two dimensions,
Drained to black and white.

And then the travelling
Scintillations begin...

Perhaps they are necklaces
Poured out of a jewellery box

As glass or diamond or river of pearl;
Maybe helical chains

Unchained from each other,
Skeins of buzzing asterisks,

And under it all the throb
Of a jagged star.

The Witch's Tongue

The moment she got the ox tongue home,
She gave it a good clubbing
With her old school hockey stick

To tenderise that combative member,
And scarified the skin
With a wire brush.

Then for the whole of one moonless night,
She drowned it and she skimmed the scum
And boiled the beast afresh.

I will not speak
Of bits and pieces of vegetables
That roiled in the changing tides,

Nor the great iron spike employed
To gouge the tongue from its root.
Suffice it to say a bond

Of old port wine and gelatine
Was integrating the elements
And a hulking boulder,

Propped on top,
Forbidding resurrection.
I cannot say

At what stage in the proceedings
The more or less handsome prince
Came striding up from the blustery foreshore.

He knocked three times
On the bungalow door,
Then pushed it open, like a familiar,

Which – being engaged
To the witch's daughter –
In fact he was.

And JESUS CHRIST THE RIGHTEOUS!
The storm-force stench that met him
Lifted him off his feet.

From the seething stove and the heaving ocean,
The clash of brine on brine!
Head-on salinities!

A stinging smart
Bitterly filled the little dwelling
And cramped his gut…

How could he marry into this?

And yet at the wedding feast,
There sat his mother-in-law:
An ivory carving with beautiful hollows

Ghosting her cheeks. And beside him,
His own bride, who'd eventually
Thought she'd give him a try.

The moon, of course,
At last consented
To flood the two-shot

With pure romance. It saw
The lovers feeding each other
Slivers of that tender gift

Pressed by her mother's hand.
It was not tart, it was not sour,
But smacked of a curious plumskin vigour

Entrancing to the senses,
With naturally, a pinch of salt
For tongue on tingling tongue.

Arthur Spark Steps Out in the Cause of Science

I step out from the old
abode where I abide

and monitor the wind's
performance indicators

well I'm blowed

it cannot be denied
it blows along the road

I take a reading
of the episode

before once more
or then again

with science on my side
I emulate the tide

and roll back
with the wind behind

where formerly I've rolled
to find

the old abode once more
the old

abode where I abide

Gordon and Walter Press Their Suits in Vain

GORDON

    The chestnut tree had dismantled its candelabra,
    Barbara,
    The hawthorn tree was no longer the queen of the may,
    When I heard that you'd moved from Scarborough to Market Harborough,
    Barbara,
    And it seemed such a very long way.

    And since you've been gone, each day's been a dismal day.
    The winter wind is chill and the skies are grey,
    And until you return from Market Harborough to Scarborough,
    Barbara,
    I don't anticipate anything being OK.

CHORUS

    He doesn't anticipate anything being OK.

BARBARA

    I moved to the Midlands to take up a post as Warden,
    Gordon,
    Of a Theological College looped and bound
    In a cordon, as it were, of the River Jordan,
    Gordon,
    And it suits me down to the ground.

    And since I arrived each day's been a lovely day.
    I feel contentment has finally come to stay,
    And I don't wish to broaden the scope of my duties as Warden,
    Gordon,
    By bringing your sensibilities into play.

CHORUS

    She won't bring his sensibilities into play.

So Gordon resolved to adopt a different policy.
He decided at once to return to his wife in Wallasey.
And he felt that fate was making sadistic fun of him
When she roundly declared that she was having *none of him*.

So Gordon walked by the sea-wall in his gloom.
He asked it why and he heard its answering boom:
Son, you've been done by the rogering todger of doom!

CHORUS

    Son, you've been done by the rogering todger of doom!

(*Enter* WALTER *and* BRENDA)

WALTER

    I hear on the grapevine you're building a hacienda,
    Brenda.
    I understand most of the major construction is done,
    But among the addenda by which you've enlarged the agenda,
    Brenda,
    Is an Aztec-style 'god of the sun'.

    Oh grant that my own be the image in which it is made!
    And mine be the features that shine on the cavalcade
    Of your natural days – in a blaze of celestial splendour,
    Brenda,
    And beam at you out of the blue – or indeed the shade!

BRENDA

    I hardly know which to regard as the major defaulter,
    Walter,
    Your balls or your brain, they're so closely bound up in deceit.
    But till you've a halter constricting your neck, you won't alter,
    Walter,
    So let us not bother to meet.

For unlike the sun, you afford neither light nor heat,
And as for the god, you're not worthy to wash his feet,
For the earth is his altar, the singing sky is his psalter,
Walter…
And I find that his music is sweet, your defeat complete!

Welcome to the Expatriate Community

I see you're reading a book. You must be new here.
Of course there's nothing wrong with reading, exactly.
It's just it isn't really what people do here,
And if you'll forgive me for putting it matter-of-factly,

Cut it out. Let me give you a tiny clue here
Concerning what's acceptable and what's not:
No one will mind if you die. It's what people do here,
Sometimes quite a lot of us on the trot.

And being a crook's OK. We've had one or two here –
In fact, come to think of it, we've had quite a few here –
They tend to be highly regarded for knowing what's what
And wielding political clout. Though one of them got

Rather beyond himself and had to be shot,
So unpleasantness can't be avoided. It's what people do here
When they feel it's time for a change in the old top slot.
You're reading a book. We'd rather you did not.

TWO

Slow Train

Slowly the slow train pulls away
To run beside the river bed
With everything I long to say
To people who are long since dead.

Torpedo Path

SS *Persia* was a P&O passenger liner on the Empire Run from Tilbury to Bombay. On 30 December 1915, 70 miles south of Crete, she was torpedoed by German U-38 under the command of Max Valentiner.

Of the 519 crew and passengers aboard 343 were lost, including my mother's mother, Joyce, and her second child, Christine (a few months). Joyce had made the journey from Bombay (Mumbai), where she lived, to her mother's home in Derbyshire in order to have the baby there. Now she was travelling with her back to India. Her first-born, my mother, Mary Beatrice, she had brought from Bombay and left in England to be brought up by her grandmother.

The *Persia* went down in 5 to 10 minutes. The sinking was especially contentious in that no warning was given as naval international law, perhaps rather optimistically, required in the case of merchant shipping carrying passengers. There was a sequence of motivation that resulted in the strike. First of all, Lieutenant Commander Godfrey Herbert, a Q-ship captain, was among those outraged by the loss of the *Lusitania* on 5 April. He found an opportunity for reprisal on 19 August when he was allegedly responsible for the murders of U-27's survivors, including its captain, Bernd Wegener. Wegener was Käpitan Leutnant Max Valentiner's cousin, close friend and comrade-in-arms. It is thought that from this point on Valentiner became implacably vengeful.

The treasure of the Maharajah of Kapurthala is maintained, it seems wrongly, to have been on board.

The eyewitness account quoted in Section 5 is taken from *A Short History of World War I* by Gary Sheffield.

1 *Mary Beatrice*

There was a baby born on Malabar Hill
    And her father was an engineer on the railway line
From Bombay to Poona, that cut through the Western Ghats,
    And the home was happy and the household gods benign.

Nevertheless there rose on Malabar Hill
    A Tower of Silence where corpses lay in a ring
And Zoroastrian vultures tore out the flesh
    And stuffed their crops and when replete, took wing.

The bones they couldn't swallow they dropped from the sky
    And they rattled and pinged on the balconies below.
This sound was among the first of the childhood memories
    Of the engineer's little daughter, as I happen to know.

But I do not know, because I neglected to ask her,
    If she recalled the banyan's cathedral shade
And aerial roots, or the sweet flowers of ashoka,
    The sorrowless tree, that lit her as she played.

Her name was Mary Beatrice, her mother's Joyce.
    And it came that Beatrice sickened and would have died
But for her ayah. She couldn't live with the climate,
    And Joyce was pregnant again, so they had to decide

What best to do. Now Joyce had a mother in England,
    All on her own and half a world away.
So she announced she'd be taking Beatrice to live there -
    Where she'd have the baby, then sail with it home to Bombay.

Well, colonial grafters and Anglo-Indians made
    The Empire Run routinely. P&O
Sailing time was about three weeks. There was nothing
    Whatever strange in Joyce's planning to go

Except for a war. A war was on. Not yet
    Entitled Great nor, plainly, Word War One,
It appeared both tragic and also an inconvenience
    To those in a continent where it hadn't begun.

But the Indian Army, they knew, was deployed and dying
    Right from the start – Tanganyika, Uganda, Baghdad
And Ypres. Still, war news tending to be a rumour
    That interwove the false with the good and the bad,

There was not much certain. But also: no time to lose,
    And Joyce and Beatrice set sail according to plan,
Safely this once, but shadowed. For Joyce and the life
    In her travelling womb, the end of life began.

2 *Joyce*

Suppose her perhaps an independent-
spirited kind of girl, Joyce Minnitt,

(a touch, maybe, headstrong,
a tinge, maybe, wilful)

and possibly more than a little hacked off
with bridge and gossip and chota pegs

and running the house and the round of routine –
and up for some sort of *adventure*?

And could there even have been a thought
of solidarity with the belligerent

homeland in its time of trouble?
To play a part, by a brush with danger,

survive it, come home with a tale to tell
to the bridge table, victorious?

And if so, why not?

3 *Wilhelm*

There was a boy who had a withered arm.
It hung there like a permanent reproach
And he was tortured at the posture farm
And put through horrors by his riding coach.
Romantically devoted to his mother,
His need was to supplant her motherland
Whose hulking navy bullied every other.
He'd cut it down to size with his good hand.

And so it came that Bismarck got the boot.
Von Tirpitz rose and poured into his ear
A dream of Ocean Dominance. Pursuit
Of this became his fixative idea.
But when the war-cloud hardened into fate,
He wanted to retract. It was too late.

4 *Maharajah*

Now the Maharajah of Kapurthala
Was a Prince of Price:

He'd as many wives as Henry VIII
And was just as nice.

And the Maharajah of Kapurthala
Was a Francophile:

In the Punjab he built himself a Palace
In Versailles style.

For the Mahajarah
Was of wealth untold:

With his elephants
And his gems and gold,

He was slated to join the ship at Marseille
But he didn't show. Did he stay away
Because he knew the last act of the play?

Maybe.

Did his treasure, without him, find a berth
In the strongroom, all those millions worth,
A hoard that went with him over the earth

And the sea?

Well, not very likely. Nobody saw
One glint of it. All that came ashore
Was the strongroom's solid, mocking door …

And farewell from the Maharajah…

65

5 *Blockade*

The far, the long, the distant, the Absolute Blockade,
That cut off the whole of the North Sea, likewise the English Channel –
And thus the entire Atlantic Ocean –

Was brought into being, was it not,
To kill the economies of the Central Powers
And starve as many civilians
As possible to death?

Which was, perhaps, a War Crime,
But very successful in the event.
No food, no clothes, no fuel in freezing winters,
No *raison d'être*, no hope.

So what could the enemy do? They had
Their *unterseebooten*, rangier
And fitter, and more resourceful
Than English submarines, though still
Sardine cans. And their crews
Better and longer trained
And more experienced fighters:
Their ace commanders were heroes
In the manner of fighter pilots
In the World War yet to come.

And so,

Not formally adopted yet
But mortally in place,
*Unrestricted Submarine
Warfare* was the tactic
And anything God suffered to move
On the waters was fair game.

Which was, perhaps, a War Crime,
But very successful in the event
So down went the passenger liners:
The *Lusitania* off Kinsale
And seven months later the *Persia*
Seventy miles off Crete.

By the way,

When a horse dropped dead in the street in Berlin
'in an instant', the eyewitness says,
'as though they'd been lying in ambush,
women armed with kitchen knives
stormed out of the apartment buildings
and fell upon the cadaver.
They screamed and hit one another
to get the best pieces
as the steaming blood sprayed their faces.'

Aboard the *Persia*,
At ten past one on the day before New Year's Eve.
Lunch was about to be served to the passengers.
Popping of corks, cooking smells …
Underneath in that otherworld
U-38,
Kapitänleutnant Max Valentiner,
After a final routine
Appraisal through the periscope,

Passed sentence on the company.

6 *Vendetta*

Valentiner and Wegener,
    Cousins, close as can be,
Were U-boat skippers in the Western Approaches,
    The North and the Irish Sea.

They hunted down merchant shipping
    In a ruthless ocean sweep,
But not till lifeboats had taken off the crews
    Did they drown it in the deep.

For Cruiser Rules of engagement
    Were unequivocal law,
And both of the combatants kept that faith
    When first they went to war.

But a pattern older than rulebooks,
    Inexorable and true,
Was the ancient spiral of vengeance, winding
    Down like the thread of a screw

Till it found the point of requital,
    As it never could fail to do,
And retaliation by retaliation,
    The dark god had his due.

Commander Godfrey Herbert
    Was a shadowing nemesis.
He counted himself insulted
    By U-boats taking the piss

With their effortless-seeming score-rate
    Of hits on the merchant fleet –
And the Dreadnoughts hiding in Scapa Flow
    In permanent retreat:

Those hulking British battleships
  That barely came into play,
Since U-boats, scenting their prey like sharks,
  Would have taken them right away...

So Q-ships, wolves in sheeps' clothing,
  Were the answer, Godfrey said.
They were dressed up as old tramp steamers,
  But armed for the kill instead.

When the passenger ship *Lusitania*
  Was holed on the starboard side
Eleven miles off the Old Head of Kinsayle,
  Twelve hundred people died.

Godfrey looked at the bodies
  Washed up by the sea,
Men and women and children and babies
  Laid out on the quay.

It wasn't a cousin who killed them –
  U-20 had made the hit –
But Godfrey promised no clemency
  And the fuse of hate was lit.

In a Q-ship called the *Baralong*,
  However, it seemed his fate
Always to miss the intended kill –
  Pitching up too late.

On that clunky old galumpher
  With his disaffected crew,
He'd nevertheless three twelve-pounder guns,
  Mountings hidden from view.

And at last 'on a beautiful calm day'
    The hex on him was broken:
He was flying neutral American colours,
    Peace's authentic token,

When he chanced on U-27 letting
    A freighter's crew go free…
So three guns roared and the U-boat men
    Were floundering in the sea …

Or they tried to climb up. From the *Baralong*
    They shot the whole crew dead
And the U-boat commander, Bernd Wegener,
    Took a bullet through the head.

Max Valentiner heard the news
    Of the murder. Compassion gone,
He made a pact with the hungry sea.
    No mercy from now on.

7 *Hit*

When Valentiner slipped the leash
And gave it its head,
How well they were all performing inside the torpedo:

The loyal flywheel
Purred and whirred in the gyroscope,
Keeping the enterprise on song:

The cold-compression engine
Roared at the shaft that spun the propeller
That hacked a freeway through the temperate waters

And Whitehead's Secret
(Of pendulum-hydrostat
Combinational pivoting)

Rode in triumphant tandem
For the creature with the dolphin nose
And the warhead in its brain.

U-BOOTE HERAUS

Did part of him resemble
A fond father at a swimming gala
Watching his talented offspring
Take the prize again?

Or was it entirely hate and glee and vengeance
And professional satisfaction

And relief?

U-BOOTE HERAUS

The second it touched the water
Many things were written
And nothing could be unmade:

For instance there stood

A three-year-old on a Castleton street
Saying to strangers *My mummy's gone to heaven
With my sister.*

Before the hit, that scene was already
Ineluctable: with the first white feather
Of spray that made the wake and the furrow

As Valentiner
Stared through the slit
And didn't breathe
Though he couldn't miss.

And many were swept away as though they were nothing,
For it came that the *Persia* began to rise on her side
Like a giantess from sleep, like a mountain wall,
Before going down stern-first:

With many bestowed a final
Lurching frame of sea or sky
And ten minutes later, she was gone.

And it further came that a salvage company,
Ninety years on and a mile and a quarter down,
Probed the Hellenic Trench
And struck the wreck again. They too
Had high-performance equipment:

Plasma rope that could lift three thousand tons
Of salvage at one go
From the back of a small ship.

They did not find
The Maharajah's gold
And they could not know the ghosts,
Among so many,
Of a baby girl or a young woman,
Loving and courageous,
Doing what was best,
As she thought it,
For her family.

8 *Tilt*

Almost amidships under the funnels
The forward boiler was hit direct
And instantly exploded. So the crew
Of engine-room and stokehold died at once,
Cremated in the roaring ghat.

Meanwhile, after the sudden
Violation,
Clout and shudder
Along the backbone of the ship
(Too loud, too likely, not to be what it was)
Calmly the women led the way
Out of the dining-room. 'Like leaving church'
One later said.

So just as in yesterday's rehearsal
Mothers were set to claim
Their children from the nursery:
All the company to retrieve
Life-belts from their cabins,
Then head for the boat stations.

But the tilt was insupportable –
Looming to starboard, portside plunging,
Now an impossible
Dancing as they
Fought to grip.

Life-boats jammed tight in the davits
And never launched:
Boats turned turtle
On their way to the water:
Empty boats rode
Clear of the ship,
Still moving fast,

And as she heeled over,
Seething gouts of ash plunged out of the funnels:
The blind propeller, half-out of the sea,
Had kept on thrashing its screwdriver circuit,
Sending up towering plumes of water
Before she rolled …

And soon it was silent for most as their heads went under,
Soon it was silence from most as their throats went under
For ever: mothers and babies,
Children and nuns,
Soldiers returning to duty,
Busy rice-dealers and millers of jute,
Entrepreneurs of the Empire,
Mechanics and missionaries, YMCA,
Nurses and ayahs:
Silence for most and likewise

The company of stokers and trimmers and firemen,
Stewards and stewardesses and storekeepers;
Maritime surgeon, butcher and baker,
Tindals, serangs and waiters and barmen;
Electricians and boilermakers,
Scullions, Marconi men, engineers;
Deckhands, Able Bodied Seamen –

Wrenched away to become the whirlpool,
Cancelled with their mass of intentions,
Dipped in oblivion just this
Single time of trying…

9 *Survivor*

And so the child that Joyce had left for good,
Mary Beatrice, lone babe in the wood,

Put her small weight against the big oak door
Which opened. She ran down the empty hall,

Calling her mother's name for evermore.

Abandoned Snooker Table

Pale with age, its green baize almost grey
Under the hanging lamps, the table rides
The shadows of the lost hotel and guides
The light to fingerprints of ancient play.
Beyond the crumbling sash the moon's in balk,
High in the summer trees. The night awaits
An outcome as the ghost deliberates...
Slow trimming of a tip with sky-blue chalk.
And then the dark manoeuvre's under way,
The hand-made viaduct, the dreaming arm
That executes its vision, plays the shot.
For here they lived and died, endured dismay
Or tasted triumph; kissed a lucky charm
Or clocked the bad unravelling of the plot.

Bookeries

They're often NEW AND SECOND-HAND
These days and it's the second-hand
That turns back time. When I was small,
Round-eyed with wonder, I'd ascend,
Behind my father, stairs that creaked
In buildings wholly occupied
By books and books. A bookery
Would be a fit name for their roost:
Also, the minor crooning sounds
Of satisfaction and surprise
The customers emitted seemed
A woodland strain of sorts. I passed
Old leather bindings, some as frail
As earthen river-cliffs, while some
Gleamed in their umber garrisons
With gold leaf medals on broad chests.
Both powder blue and faded rose
Were singing colours on the decks,
The landings and the terraces,
In standing coffins, catafalques
Of books and books and books. I duly
Followed the coconut matting road –
Or trail of lino, threadbare cloth –
The mealy, malty, nutty, dusty
Scent of reading till we found
The denizen within his den:
His coins in a tobacco tin,
His notes elastic-banded. There,
A small transaction. So outside,
And sweets for me. And then the bus,
On which my father tried the weight
And character of those *trouvailles*,
Spreading the volumes on his knee,
His modest treasures borne safe home.

A Night on the Tiles

(In the *Dolphin* pub in Hackney, a Victorian mosaic
depicts the story of Arion the musician and the dolphin
which saved his life by rescuing him from sea-robbers
and carrying him on its back to Tanairos.)

The poet sits at the bar of the *Dolphin*
And takes his ease
With difficulty.

For sorrow assails him and even his creamy black jar
Of stout may not avail.
Deficient in serenity,

He mopes by the mythological mosaic,
Whose glaze displays a bard
Superior in glory.

He mopes but in a while rehearses
Transcendental hopes:

> *Arion, Arion, songsmith Arion,*
> *mean lyre-player and plectro-daedalist,*
> *kithara maestro, dithyrambunctious*
> *Dionysian on the salt sea:*

> *Arion, play for me!*

The poet stands by the bar of the *Dolphin*.
He takes his ease
With difficulty.

For he is by no means confident that the bard
Will oblige, and is keenly sensible
Of his own inferiority.

For though he has won poetry prizes,
No one has therefore tried to kill him
Nor has he charmed

Intended murderers with his song,
Or used it to summon a dolphin
To carry him home

> *Over the foam:*
> *Arion, Arion, songsmith Arion,*
> *mean lyre-picker and plectro-daedalist,*
> *kithara maestro, dithyrambunctious*
> *singer-songwriter on the salt sea:*
>
> *Arion, play for me!*

And curiously,
The empty pub fills with shadow dancers
Lapping the hollow island of the bar
As they execute their antistrophe.

And above them, raucous, vinous,
Yet freighted with an independent grace,
What should it be but a killer
Lyric to the lyre?

The Eyes of Mr Silverman

A giant wooden pair of spectacles –
a thirties pair like wheels of rolling stock –
hung high above the premises
of little Mr Silverman,
community optician for a full quintet of decades,
putting Hackney's peepers through their paces.

Oh reinstate the hard oak chairs
that backed the wall of the waiting room
while at the centre of the piece,
cushioned and comfortable, sat Ruth,
the practice's receptionist,
quite often in her woolly hat with earflaps,
abstractedly benign.

Ladies would drop in from the street
and take the seat beside her
and tell her the story of their lives
and their relative's lives
and their friends' lives
and Ruth sustained an understanding hum…

Jacket and tie and old-time corduroys,
and watch-chain, so I seem to remember
(though maybe I romance)
accoutred Mr Silverman
in the exercise of his mystery
within the darkened sanctum. And of course,

no computer.
An apothecary cabinet
kept safe the peculiar vision of each client,
noted in his looping hand.
Now he is irreplaceable
and the place is irreplaceable

and in place of the wooden spectacles,
in tribute to Mr Silverman
the mind's eye stations a modest flame
(to his expertise, to his friendliness),
small, distinct, uncompromised
and so far, not extinguished.

Rat-Rhymes for Unfamiliars

Dabblers in the Occult
Cannot be certain
Of an interesting result.

Scientific support
Is nil for a thesis
Of Telekinesis,

Nor can be found empirical
Evidence
Of Miracle.

Numbers of those with faith
In Spoon-bending
Are descending

Pending
An ending
To the profession outright.

Spoon-
Benders,
Goodnight.

Yet WE WOULD HAVE A SIGN:
A simple spasm
Of ectoplasm

Would suffice;
In fact, would be nice.
But not at any price

Will Life administer
One seedling
Of the sinister

In the form of, say, a Ghost
(Which is what we'd like most).
The Rector?

No use.
He's failed to produce
A Spectre.

The Medium?
Induces
Tedium.

The Supernatural
And the Paranormal
Combine in a way

Disappointingly
Formal:
THE SUPERNORMAL.

Which is well understood
As being no earthly
Unearthly good.

A Sentimental Education

Son, that's how it was, we were raised
To know the value of hard work:
Nothing. Likewise

The absolute power
Of appropriation. Want it,
You'd better take it,

No one'll give it you.
Except, of course, for the dear old twins
Who'd give you their last cup of sugar

For a bent copper, those were the days.
I can see it now,
Ronnie putting my brother

Through ballet school and Reggie,
Out of the goodness of his heart,
Beating me up in the club bog. My son,

In those days we policed ourselves,
We had our own prisons and torture chambers –
It was Them and Us –

And It, I seem to remember.
It, I seem to remember.
Though somehow I can't remember
What that was.

Just Before the Ruination

(a late August lament)

It's like the ocean's plain of blues
Modulating from turquoise out to midnight,
Scrolling from beach to horizon
Where sails are spaced like thorns along a rose-branch.

Only,
This is of course the green range: madam,
Acid acacia through
To malachite on to spinachy iron:
Every green in the book at the end of the summer.

And the whole thing is perilous
But it wants to make a stand
For the panoply of freedoms
About to go.

The great earth-works will do no good:
The chlorophyll silos
Tremble like a child's lip,
Like a pan of water about to boil.

They realise their betrayal.

Nevertheless
The fine rain falls,
Preserving what it can while yet it may.
The fine and feeling rain
Nurses their dying as though it were the beginning.

The Gulls

That August afternoon as she lay dying
   They were nowhere near the sea
But gangs of gulls were trashing the sky with screams
   Inordinately, unconscionably,
   In rival screams replying.

Nowhere near the sea.
   He thought she might be confused
And he didn't want her to be
   Confused by the gulls' crying.

So he told her how they had swung round from the river,
   From salt-marsh or mud-flat,
After a garbage bonanza. He kept talking garbage
   Of gulls, the black-backed, the common, the herring,
   Of which he knew little. Then he sat sighing

Most of that August afternoon
   Until the gulls had flown
   As she lay dreaming,
   And as she lay dying.

Dancing to 'Slough'

Back from the broken urinal
When the party was in its last throes,
She took in the soft gleam of vinyl
And the lyric that from it arose.

Then she further observed from a corner
Through the number's impossible gloom
The floor's only resident fauna,
A couple commanding the room,

Who were strangely engaged there somehow:
    Dan...cing...to...'Slough'.

They seemed more like sister and brother
Than lovers – still more like tombstones
As they propped themselves up on each other
Over the poem's sad bones.

The candles were flinching and flickery.
They cast a mad light on the floor
To words which weren't made for Terpsichore:
They'd never been danced to before,

So why was it happening now:
    Dan...cing...to...'Slough'?

Well, it wasn't *commedia dell arte*,
No drama whatever unfurled,
But it signalled the end of the party
And also the end of the world...

So she left them with barely a *ciao*,
    Dan...cing...to...'Slough'...

Last Chorus

a classics teacher in age

Sing me the rivers of hell, boys,
Sing me the rivers of hell.

Lay down the last of them classical riffs
And row me home with the old-time stiffs

By Lethe, Cocytus, Acheron, Styx
And Phlegethon –

That's Megathon –

So sing them loud and well.
I'll hear you clear as a bell

Down by the banks where the grey souls wander
The meadows of asphodel…

And there's nothing left to tell.
Last chorus:

Sing me the rivers of hell.

Caneback: A Phantasmagoria

founded on Trollope's The American Senator

All night long and all night long

The foxes were barking for Major Caneback
To pull up his boots and hit the road:
The rough road out of the Brake Country
On the bad mare that had rolled on his body
And kicked in his head as he crawled from the ditch.

Well, a dying man is always a living man
Too – the Major kept going through dream,
Riding one-armed, his shoulder broken,
On the rough road out of this world in his sleep.
And they'd carried him back on a door from the hunting field,

Laid him down, to expire in a guest room;
Way down the shadowy, echoey corridor,
High above the ballroom where strings were beginning.
For the dance goes on whoever is dying:
Radiance, gallantry, polka-mazurkas,

Roses, and oak floors beeswaxed to ebony;
Pale yellow wallpaper, laughter, champagne.
Now partners bowing, the long lines running
The length of the room and the lane down the middle…
While up above them, in his last roughhouse

Under the cave wall, streaming with shadows,
The Major wrestled with the Angel of Death.
And when he was done for, his spirit tipped
From alembic to crucible to roaring chasm,
One more time he arose in the darkness.

One more time they melded together,
He and the mare, the only creature
He'd ever failed to break in his life.
They were revenants now in combination
As the rocking shape came on down the corridor;

Slamming portraits off the walls,
Crashing doorframes, leaping the landing;
Stamping on to the slithering dance-floor,
Screams of the dancers rising to meet them,
Taking the wall as they took the darkness,

Mare and Major's last goodnight...

St Bernard and the Blackbird

As Bernard was preaching one day by God's grace,
An impudent blackbird flew into his face.

In contradistinction to tender St Francis,
St Bernard rejected the blackbird's advances.

Divine inspiration dictated his course:
He seized it and tore off its wings by main force.

'And that is the last time,' he said to the bird,
'The last time you fly in the face of God's word.'

Though the faithful assert that the story is true,
You cannot imagine the reason they do –

But they seem to be proud of St Bernard's display:
Surely a psychopath having his way.

Drink So Much Whiskey I Stagger When I'm Sleep

Sometimes nothing would do
but the jug band from the swamp
stomping the dirt road
down the bayou
grunting bass and wailing mouth-harp
chain-gang holler and low moon riding
the cypress trees

hauling along that long-time sorrow
crying out in that strange joy
sometimes nothing else

could hope to bring it home